Inspiring Words to Live By

The Little Book of Meditation Quotes

**Edited by
Kathleen Welton**

Copyright ©2021 aka associates, inc.
All rights reserved.

The Little Book of Meditation Quotes is available at special discounts when purchased in quantities for educational use, fund-raising or sales promotions. Special editions or book excerpts can also be created. For more information, please contact: info@akabooks.com.

Book design by Zaccarine Design, Inc.

ISBN-10: 0-578-87466-0
ISBN-13: 978-0-578-87466-1

www.akabooks.com

Contents

- iv Thank You
- v Introduction
  - ❋ Aware 1
  - ❋ Calm 9
  - ❋ Creative 17
  - ❋ Grateful 25
  - ❋ Happy 33
  - ❋ Healthy 43
  - ❋ Hopeful 53
  - ❋ Patient 61
  - ❋ Peaceful 71
  - ❋ Purposeful 79
  - ❋ Resilient 89
  - ❋ Thoughtful 99
- 111 Appendix: Favorite Meditation Quotes
- 115 Appendix: Meditation Checklist
- 121 Appendix: Meditation Journal
- 125 Biographical Index
- 129 Index
- 133 About the Author

Thank You

This book wouldn't exist without the help
and encouragement of many people.

First and foremost, thank you to the authors of
these quotes—whose words have stood the
test of time over many years.

Second, I am grateful to many others including
Herbert Benson, MD, Jack Kornfield, Thich Nhat
Hanh, Jon Kabat-Zinn, and Andrew Weil, MD, whose audio
programs, books, courses, music, research, and other
materials inspired my own meditation
journey more than a decade ago.

Third, thanks to all those who shine a light for others to follow with their words and actions.

And finally, I am grateful to my cats Ava, Lana, Little
Caesar, Sassy, and Simba who have been my constant
companions and Zen masters throughout my journey.

Introduction

This is a collection of 365 meditation quotes—a quote to use as inspiration for each day of the year. Quotes have been selected to cover a dozen topics. They are arranged for easy access as follows to be:

- ❋ Aware
- ❋ Calm
- ❋ Creative
- ❋ Grateful
- ❋ Happy
- ❋ Healthy
- ❋ Hopeful
- ❋ Patient
- ❋ Peaceful
- ❋ Purposeful
- ❋ Resilient
- ❋ Thoughtful

The quotes are arranged alphabetically by author in each section, so that you can easily find your favorite quotes by topic and by author. Some of the quotes were collected over the years. Others were researched and selected specifically for this book.

Regarding meditation, I am reminded of the following Zen story: A martial arts student went to his teacher and said earnestly, "I am devoted to studying your martial system. How long will it take me to learn?" The teacher's reply was casual, "Ten years." Impatiently, the student answered, "But I want to master it faster than that. I will work very hard. I will practice every day, ten or more hours a day if I have to. How long will it take then?" The teacher thought for a moment, "20 years."

My goal for this project has been to bring some light into your life whenever you open these pages. I hope that you will find these quotes to be inspiring for you and your journey—no matter where you may *be* on it.

>Namaste!

>Kathleen Welton
>April 2021

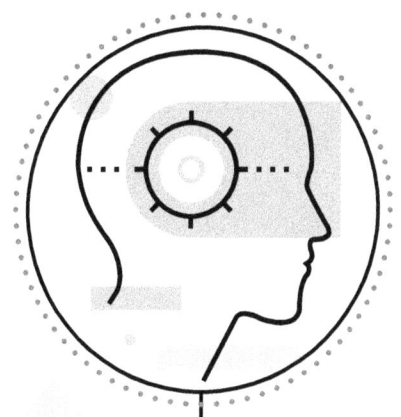

Aware

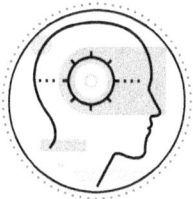

Quality is not an act, it is a habit.

~ Aristotle

⌘

We are what we repeatedly do.
Excellence, then, is not an act, but a habit.

~ Aristotle

⌘

Don't go on discussing what a
good person should be.
Just be one.

~ Marcus Aurelius

⌘

Look within. Within is the fountain of good,
and it will ever bubble up, if thou wilt ever dig.

~ Marcus Aurelius

⌘

Natural abilities are like natural plants;
they need pruning by study.

~ *Francis Bacon*

⌘

Judge not, that ye be not judged.

~ *Bible, Matthew 7:1*

⌘

To see a World of Grain of Sand
And Heaven in a Wild Flower.
Hold Infinity in the palm of your hand
And Eternity in an hour.

~ *William Blake*

⌘

My actions are my only belongings.
I cannot escape the consequences of my actions.
My actions are the ground on which I stand.

~ *Buddha*

⌘

You yourself, as much as anybody in the entire universe,
deserve your love and affection.

~ *Buddha*

⌘

The merit of all things lies in their difficulty.
~ *Alexandre Dumas*

⌘

The first condition of human
goodness is something to love;
the second something to reverence.
~ *George Eliot*

⌘

People only see what they are prepared to see.
~ *Ralph Waldo Emerson*

⌘

What I need is someone who will
make me do what I can.
~ *Ralph Waldo Emerson*

⌘

First, say to yourself what you would be;
and then do what you have to do.
~ *Epictetus*

⌘

The key is to keep company only with people who
uplift you, whose presence calls forth your best.

~ Epictetus

⌘

An awake heart is like a sky that pours light.

~ Hafez

⌘

The noblest pleasure is the joy of understanding.

~ Leonardo da Vinci

⌘

Why does the eye see a thing more clearly
in dreams than the imagination when awake?

~ Leonardo da Vinci

⌘

Even a thought, even a possibility,
can shatter and transform us.

~ Friedrich Nietzsche

⌘

Behind an able man there are always other able men.

~ Chinese Proverb

⌘

Everyone must row with the oars he has.

~ *English Proverb*

⌘

Don't be satisfied with stories,
how things have gone with others.
Unfold your own myth.

~ *Rumi*

⌘

The quieter you become,
the more you are able to hear.

~ *Rumi*

⌘

You were born with wings,
why prefer to crawl through life?

~ *Rumi*

⌘

Whatever you are, try to be a good one.

~ *William Makepeace Thackeray*

⌘

Being is the great explainer.

~ *Henry David Thoreau*

⌘

Everyone thinks about changing the world,
but no one thinks about changing himself.

~ Leo Tolstoy

⌘

Is it true? Is it kind? Is it worth saying?

~ Author Unknown

⌘

You will begin to heal when you let go of past hurts.
Forgive those who have wronged you and
learn to forgive yourself for your mistakes.

~ Author Unknown

⌘

The key to growth is the introduction of higher
dimensions of consciousness into our awareness.

~ Lao Tzu

⌘

I exist as I am, that is enough,
If no other in the world be aware I sit content,
And if each and all be aware I sit content.

~ Walt Whitman

⌘

Calm

It is necessary for the perfection of human society that there should be men who devote their loves to contemplation.

~ *Saint Thomas Aquinas*

⌘

The nearer a man comes to a calm mind, the closer he is to strength.

~ *Marcus Aurelius*

⌘

Be like a tree in pursuit of your cause.
Stand firm, grip hard,
Thrust upward,
bend to the winds of heaven,
and learn tranquility.

~ *Dedication to Richard St. Barbe Baker, Father of the Trees*

⌘

Be still, and know that I am God;
I will be exalted among the nations,
I will be exalted in the earth!

~ *Bible, Psalm 46:10*

⌘

Do not learn how to react.
Learn how to respond.

~ *Buddha*

⌘

Temperance is a tree which as
for its root very little contentment,
and for its fruit calm and peace.

~ *Buddha*

⌘

When you realize how perfect everything is
you will tilt your head back and laugh at the sky.

~ *Buddha*

⌘

There are some things you learn best in calm,
and some in storm.

~ *Willa Cather*

⌘

Calm

There is pleasure in calm
remembrance of a past sorrow.

~ Cicero

⌘

Our storm is past, and that storm's tyrannous rage,
A stupid calm, but nothing it, doth 'suage.

~ John Donne

⌘

Be not the slave of your own past—
plunge into the sublime seas, dive deep, and
swim far, so you shall come back with new self-respect,
with new power, and with an advanced experience
that shall explain and overlook the old.

~ Ralph Waldo Emerson

⌘

In the woods, we return to reason and faith.
There I feel that nothing can befall me in life—
no disgrace, no calamity (leaving me my eyes),
which nature cannot repair.

~ Ralph Waldo Emerson

⌘

Silence is true wisdom's best reply.

~ Euripides

⌘

Within you, there is a stillness and a sanctuary to which you can retreat at any time and be yourself.

~ Hermann Hesse

⌘

In calmness lies true pleasure.

~ Victor Hugo

⌘

Old age has a great sense of calm and freedom. When the passions have relaxed their hold and have escaped, not from one master, but from many.

~ Plato

⌘

There are two things a
person should never be angry at,
what they can help, and what they cannot.

~ Plato

⌘

Tension is who you think you should be, relaxation is who you are.

~ Chinese Proverb

⌘

In a calm sea, every man is a pilot.

~ *English Proverb*

⌘

After a storm comes a calm.

~ *Proverb*

⌘

To be calm is the highest achievement of the self.

~ *Zen Proverb*

⌘

For there is no friend like a sister
in calm or stormy weather;
To cheer one on the tedious way,
to fetch one if one goes astray,
to lift one if one totters down,
to strengthen whilst one stands.

~ *Christina Rossetti*

⌘

Listen to the sound of waves within you.

~ *Rumi*

⌘

Raise your words, not your voice.
It is rain that grows flowers, not thunder.

~ Rumi

⌘

Few things are brought to a
successful issue by impetuous desire,
but most by calm and prudent forethought.

~ Thucydides

⌘

The true strength of a man is in calmness.

~ Leo Tolstoy

⌘

Be still like a mountain and flow like a great river.

~ Lao Tzu

⌘

Make your heart like a lake,
with a calm, still surface,
and great depths of kindness.

~ Lao Tzu

⌘

Creative

Creative

All beginnings are mysteries,
the mystery of creation.
~ *Henri Frédéric Amiel*

⌘

The nearer a man comes to a calm mind,
the closer he is to strength.
~ *Marcus Aurelius*

⌘

Men are like trees: each one must put forth
the leaf that is created in him.
~ *Henry Ward Beecher*

⌘

The man of genius inspires us with a boundless
confidence in our own powers.
~ *Ralph Waldo Emerson*

⌘

To be yourself in a world that is constantly
trying to make you something else
is the greatest accomplishment.

~ *Ralph Waldo Emerson*

⌘

As soon as you trust yourself,
you will know how to live.

~ *Johann Wolfgang von Goethe*

⌘

Genius is formed in quiet,
character in the stream of human life.

~ *Johann Wolfgang von Goethe*

⌘

Stay close to anything that
makes you glad you are alive.

~ *Hafez*

⌘

Within you, there is a stillness
and a sanctuary to which you can
retreat at any time and be yourself.

~ *Hermann Hesse*

⌘

Creative

Music expresses that which cannot be put into words.

~ Victor Hugo

⌘

The knowledge of all things is possible.

~ Leonardo da Vinci

⌘

Learn how to see. Realize that everything
connects to everything else.

~ Leonardo da Vinci

⌘

The painter has the Universe in his mind and hands.

~ Leonardo da Vinci

⌘

In creating, the only hard thing's to begin;
A grass blade's no easier to make than an oak.

~ James Russell Lowell

⌘

Perfection is no small thing,
but it is made up of small things.

~ Michelangelo

⌘

When I am completely myself,
entirely alone during the night when I cannot sleep,
it is on such occasions that my ideas flow best
and most abundantly.

~ Mozart

⌘

You must have chaos within you
to give birth to a dancing star.

~ Friedrich Nietzsche

⌘

Don't be satisfied with stories,
how things have gone with others.
Unfold your own myth.

~ Rumi

⌘

All art is but imitation of nature.

~ Seneca

⌘

The divine spark lives in all of us,
and perpetually strives toward its origin.

~ Seneca

⌘

Creative

Every new beginning comes from
some other beginning's end.

~ Seneca

⌘

Invention, it must be humbly admitted,
does not consist in creating out of void but out of chaos.

~ Mary Shelley

⌘

Don't judge each day by the harvest you reap
but by the seeds that you plant.

~ Robert Louis Stevenson

⌘

The true strength of a man is in calmness.

~ Leo Tolstoy

⌘

Keep your thoughts positive and flow with life.

~ Author Unknown

⌘

If you hear a voice within you say "you cannot paint,"
then by all means paint, and that voice will be silenced.

~ Vincent van Gogh

⌘

Great things are not done by impulse,
but a series of small things brought together.

~ Vincent van Gogh

⌘

The pessimist complains about the wind;
the optimist expects it to change;
the realist adjusts the sails.

~ William Arthur Ward

⌘

An idea that is not dangerous is unworthy
of being called an idea at all.

~ Oscar Wilde

⌘

The imagination imitates.
It is the critical spirit that creates.

~ Oscar Wilde

⌘

With an eye made quiet
by the power of harmony,
and the deep power of joy,
we see into the life of things.

~ William Wordsworth

⌘

Grateful

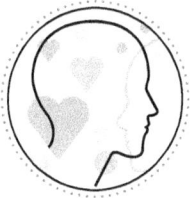

Gratitude is a sign of noble souls.

~ *Aesop*

⌘

Gratitude turns what we have into enough.

~ *Aesop*

⌘

Thankfulness is the beginning of gratitude.
Gratitude is the completion of thankfulness.
Thankfulness may consist merely of words.
Gratitude is shown in acts.

~ *Henri Frédéric Amiel*

⌘

The beauty of the soul shines out when a man bears
with composure one heavy mischance after another,
not because he does not feel them, but because
he is a man of high and heroic temper.

~ *Aristotle*

⌘

Let your speech always be gracious,
seasoned with salt,
so that you may know how you
ought to answer each person.

~ Bible, Colossians 4:6

⌘

As he thinketh in his heart, so he is.

~ Bible, Proverbs 23:7

⌘

Forget injuries, never forget kindnesses.

~ Confucius

⌘

I was complaining that I had no shoes
till I met a man who had no feet.

~ Confucius

⌘

Wear a smile and have friends;
wear a scowl and have wrinkles.

~ George Eliot

⌘

Write it on your heart hat every day
is the best day in the year.

~ *Ralph Waldo Emerson*

⌘

Let my heart be wise. It is the gods' best gift.

~ *Euripides*

⌘

May the gratitude in my heart kiss all the universe.

~ *Hafez*

⌘

Be grateful in your own hearts. That suffices.
Thanksgiving has wings, and flies
to its right destination.

~ *Victor Hugo*

⌘

Even the darkest night will end and the sun will rise.

~ *Victor Hugo*

⌘

I would rather be able to appreciate things I can not have
than to have things I am not able to appreciate.

~ *Elbert Hubbard*

⌘

I love you
I'm sorry
Please forgive me
Thank you

~ Hawaiian Mantra

⌘

The deepest craving of human nature
is the need to be appreciated.

~ William James

⌘

The essence of all beautiful art is gratitude.

~ Friedrich Nietzsche

⌘

Truly kind people forget the good
things they have done in the past.
They are so involved in the things
they do now that they forget the
things they have done before.

~ Chinese Proverb

⌘

Count your blessings.

~ Proverb

⌘

Giving thanks for abundance is
greater than the abundance itself.

~ Rumi

⌘

Wear gratitude like a cloak,
and it will feed every corner of your life.

~ Rumi

⌘

Nothing is more honorable than a grateful heart.

~ Seneca

⌘

O Lord that lends me life,
lend me a heart replete with thankfulness.

~ William Shakespeare

⌘

Clouds come floating into my life,
no longer to carry rain or usher storm,
but to add color to my sunset sky.

~ Rabindranath Tagore

⌘

A good laugh is sunshine in the house.
~ *William Makepeace Thackeray*

⌘

An early-morning walk is a
blessing for the whole day.
~ *Henry David Thoreau*

⌘

Gratitude turns what we have into enough.
~ *Author Unknown*

⌘

Appreciation is a wonderful thing.
It makes what is excellent in others
belong to us as well.
~ *Voltaire*

⌘

Rest and be thankful.
~ *William Wordsworth*

⌘

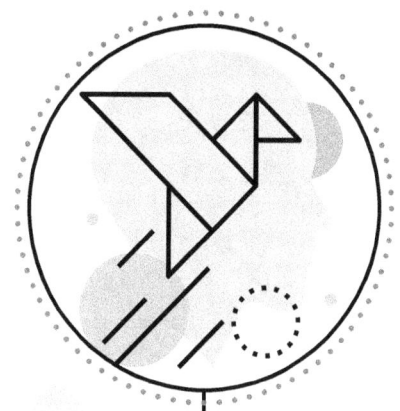

Happy

The power of finding beauty
in the humblest things makes
home happy and life lovely.

~ Louisa May Alcott

⌘

Happiness depends upon ourselves.

~ Aristotle

⌘

Happiness is an expression
of the soul in considered actions.

~ Aristotle

⌘

The happiness of your life depends upon
the quality of your thoughts.

~ Marcus Aurelius

⌘

Very little is needed to make a happy life;
it is all within yourself, in your way of thinking.

~ Marcus Aurelius

⌘

Learn to let go. That is the key to happiness.

~ Buddha

⌘

Thousands of candles can be
lighted from a single candle, and the
life of the candle will not be shortened.
Happiness never decreases by being shared.

~ Buddha

⌘

To enjoy good health, to bring true happiness
to one's family, to bring peace to all, one must
first discipline and control one's own mind.
If a man can control his mind he can find
the way to Enlightenment, and all wisdom
and virtue will naturally come to him.

~ Buddha

⌘

There are two ways to get enough.
One is to continue to accumulate more and more.
The other is to desire less.

~ *G.K. Chesterton*

⌘

And remember, no matter where you go,
there you are.

~ *Confucius*

⌘

What you do not want done to yourself,
do not do to others.

~ *Confucius*

⌘

Happiness is a gift and the trick is not to expect it,
but to delight in it when it comes.

~ *Charles Dickens*

⌘

Action may not always bring happiness;
but there is no happiness without action.

~ *Benjamin Disraeli*

⌘

For every minute you are angry
you lose sixty seconds of happiness.

~ *Ralph Waldo Emerson*

⌘

There is only one way to happiness and
that is to cease worrying about things
which are beyond the power of our will.

~ *Epictetus*

⌘

A single sunbeam is enough to
drive away many shadows.

~ *Saint Francis of Assisi*

⌘

Happiness consists more in small
conveniences or pleasures that occur every day,
than in great pieces of good fortune that happen
but seldom to a man in the course of his life.

~ *Benjamin Franklin*

⌘

Thou must gather thine own sunshine.

~ *Nathaniel Hawthorne*

⌘

If you want happiness for an hour—take a nap.
If you want happiness for a day—go fishing.
If you want happiness for a year—inherit a fortune.
If you want happiness for a lifetime—help someone else.

~ Chinese Proverb

⌘

Perhaps they are not stars,
but rather openings in heaven where the
love of our lost ones pours through and shines
down upon us to let us know they are happy.

~ Eskimo Proverb

⌘

Happiness does not come from happiness itself,
but from the journey towards achieving it.

~ Finnish Proverb

⌘

If you are too busy to laugh, you are too busy.

~ Proverb

⌘

It is more fitting for a man to laugh at life
than to lament over it.

~ Seneca

⌘

There are more things to
alar us than to harm us,
and we suffer more often in
apprehension than reality.

~ Seneca

⌘

True happiness is…to enjoy the present,
without anxious dependence upon the future.

~ Seneca

⌘

The secret of happiness? Enjoy small pleasures.

~ Samuel Smiles

⌘

Happiness consists of living each day as if
it were the first day of your honeymoon
and the last day of your vacation.

~ Leo Tolstoy

⌘

Being happy doesn't mean everything is perfect.
It means you've decided to look beyond
the imperfections.

~ Author Unknown

⌘

Don't let the world change your smile,
but let your smile change the world.

~ Author Unknown

⌘

Happiness is the art of never holding
in your mind the memory of any
unpleasant thing that has passed.

~ Author Unknown

⌘

A well-developed sense of humor is
the pole that adds balance to your steps
as you walk the tightrope of life.

~ William Arthur Ward

⌘

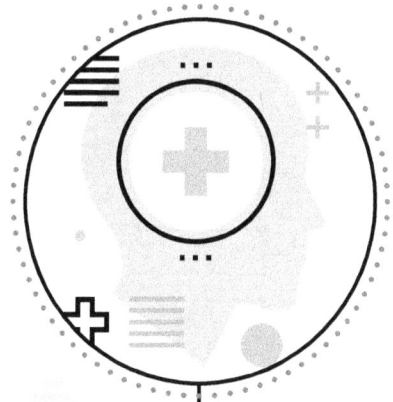

Healthy

Cheerfulness is the best promoter of health
and is as friendly to the mind as to the body.

~ Joseph Addison

⌘

The body is like a piano, and happiness is like music.
It is needful to have the instrument in good order.

~ Henry Ward Beecher

⌘

The secret of health for both mind and body is…
live the present moment wisely and earnestly.

~ Buddha

⌘

To keep the body in good health is a duty…
otherwise we shall not be able to
keep our mind strong and clear.

~ Buddha

⌘

In a disordered mind, as in a disordered body,
soundness of health is impossible.

~ *Cicero*

⌘

It is exercise alone that supports the spirits,
and keeps the mind in vigor.

~ *Cicero*

⌘

Divide each difficulty into as many parts
as is feasible and necessary to resolve it,
and watch the whole transform.

~ *René Descartes*

⌘

Prevention is better than cure.

~ *Desiderius Erasmus*

⌘

Healing is a matter of time,
but it is sometimes also a
matter of opportunity.

~ *Hippocrates*

⌘

The greatest weapon against stress is our
ability to choose one thought over another.

~ William James

⌘

We should pray for a sane mind in a sound body.

~ Juvenal

⌘

The part can never be well
unless the whole is well.

~ Plato

⌘

The secret of health for both mind
and body is not to mourn for the past,
not to worry about the future,
or not to anticipate troubles,
but to live in the present moment
wisely and earnestly.

~ Buddhist Proverb

⌘

A man grows most tired while standing still.

~ Chinese Proverb

⌘

When the heart is at ease,
the body is healthy.

~ *Chinese Proverb*

⌘

A good laugh and a long sleep
are the best cures in the doctor's book.

~ *Irish Proverb*

⌘

May the blessing of light be on you,
light without and light within.
May the blessed sunshine shine on you
and warm your heart till it
glows like a great peat fire, so that the
stranger may come and warm himself at it,
and also a friend.

~ *Traditional Irish Blessing*

⌘

Every time you feel yourself being pulled
into other people's drama, repeat these words:
Not my circus, not my monkeys.

~ *Polish Proverb*

⌘

May all things be happy.

~ Zuni Prayer

⌘

The universe and the light of the
world shine through me.

~ Rumi

⌘

The wound is the place
where the Light enters you.

~ Rumi

⌘

It is not in the stars to hold
our destiny but in ourselves.

~ William Shakespeare

⌘

Our bodies are our gardens,
to the which our wills
are our gardeners.

~ William Shakespeare

⌘

You know who you are,
but know not who you could be.

~ William Shakespeare

⌘

The really important
thing is not to live,
but to live well…
and to live well means
the same thing as to live
honourably or rightly.

~ Socrates

⌘

Good health and good sense
are two of life's greatest blessings.

~ Publilius Syrus

⌘

The biggest happiness is when at
the end of the year you feel better
than at the beginning.

~ Henry David Thoreau

⌘

Healthy

Because one believes in oneself,
one doesn't try to convince others.
Because one is content with oneself,
one doesn't need others' approval.
Because one accepts oneself,
the whole world accepts him or her.

~ Lao Tzu

⌘

Health is the greatest possession.
Contentment is the greatest treasure.
Confidence is the greatest friend.

~ Lao Tzu

⌘

I have chosen to be happy
because it is good for my health.

~ Voltaire

⌘

Hopeful

Now I know in part;
then I shall know fully,
even as I am fully known.
And now these three remain:
faith, hope, and love;
but the greatest of these is love.

~ *Bible, 1 Corinthians 13:13*

⌘

You will be secure, because there is hope;
you will look about you and take your rest in safety.

~ *Bible, Job 11:18-19*

⌘

Courage is like love;
it must have hope for nourishment.

~ *Napoleon Bonaparte*

⌘

A leader is a dealer in hope.

~ *Napoleon Bonaparte*

⌘

At first people refuse to believe
that a strange new thing can be done,
then they begin to hope it can be done,
then they see it can be done—
then it is done and all the world wonders
why it was not done centuries ago.

~ Frances Hodgson Burnett

⌘

Hope springs exulting on triumphant wing.

~ Robert Burns

⌘

Hope is the power of being cheerful in
circumstances that we know to be desperate.

~ G.K. Chesterton

⌘

While there's life, there's hope.

~ Cicero

⌘

Education breeds confidence.
Confidence breeds hope.
Hope breeds peace.

~ Confucius

⌘

To love a thing means wanting it to live.

~ *Confucius*

⌘

It's always something,
to know you've done the most you could.
But, don't leave off hoping,
or it's of no use doing anything.
Hope, hope to the last!

~ *Charles Dickens*

⌘

Hope is a strange invention—
A Patent of the Heart—
In unremitting action
Yet never wearing out—

~ *Emily Dickinson*

⌘

I am prepared for the worst,
but hope for the best.

~ *Benjamin Disraeli*

⌘

To live without hope is to cease to live.

~ *Fyodor Dostoyevsky*

⌘

This new day is too dear,
with its hopes and invitations,
to waste a moment on the yesterdays.
~ Ralph Waldo Emerson

⌘

Don't hope that events will turn out the way you want,
welcome events in whichever way they happen:
this is the path to peace.
~ Epictetus

⌘

If it were not for hopes, the heart would break.
~ Thomas Fuller

⌘

In all things it is better to hope than to despair.
~ Johann Wolfgang von Goethe

⌘

Positive anything is better than negative nothing.
~ Elbert Hubbard

⌘

There is nothing like a dream to create the future.
~ Victor Hugo

⌘

Hope is itself a species of happiness, and, perhaps,
the chief happiness which this world affords.

~ Samuel Johnson

⌘

Where there is no hope there can be no endeavour.

~ Samuel Johnson

⌘

Rules for happiness: something to do,
someone to love, something to hope for.

~ Immanuel Kant

⌘

He who plants a tree, plants a hope.

~ Lucy Larcom

⌘

Hope has as many lives as a cat or a king.

~ Henry Wadsworth Longfellow

⌘

He who has health has hope;
and he who has hope has everything.

~ Arabian Proverb

⌘

Hope is the last thing ever lost.

~ Italian Proverb

⌘

If Winter comes, can Spring be far behind?

~ Percy Bysshe Shelley

⌘

Hope
Smiles from the threshold of the year to come,
Whispering "it will be happier"…

~ Alfred Lord Tennyson

⌘

If we will be quiet and ready enough, we shall find compensation in every disappointment.

~ Henry David Thoreau

⌘

An anniversary is a time to
celebrate the joys of today,
the memories of yesterday,
and the hopes of tomorrow.

~ Author Unknown

⌘

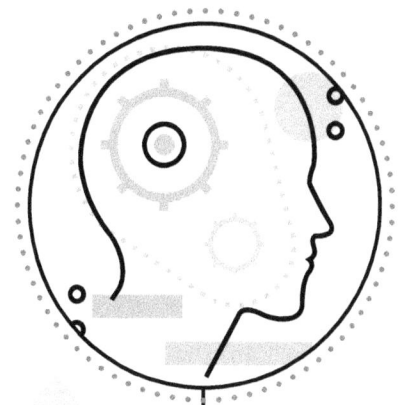

Patient

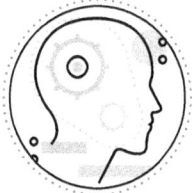

Patience and perseverance have a magical effect before which difficulties disappear and obstacles vanish.

~ John Quincy Adams

⌘

Patience is bitter, but its fruit is sweet.

~ Aristotle

⌘

Patience is the companion of wisdom.

~ Saint Augustine

⌘

Dwell on the beauty of life. Watch the stars, and see yourself running with them.

~ Marcus Aurelius

⌘

What is conceived well is expressed clearly,
And the words to say it arrive with ease.

~ Nicolas Boileau

⌘

Patience is conquering virtue.

~ Geoffrey Chaucer

⌘

Adopt the pace of nature:
her secret is patience.

~ Ralph Waldo Emerson

⌘

Patience and fortitude conquer all things.

~ Ralph Waldo Emerson

⌘

He that can have patience can have what he will.

~ Benjamin Franklin

⌘

Live each day as if your life had just begun.

~ Johann Wolfgang Von Goethe

⌘

Good character is not
formed in a week or a month.
It is created little by little, day by day.
Protracted and patient effort is
needed to develop good character.

~ Heraclitus

⌘

What would the world be, once bereft
Of wet and of Wildness? Let be left,
O let them be left, wildness and wet,
Long live the weeds and the wilderness yet.

~ Gerard Manley Hopkins

⌘

Be not afraid of life.
Believe that life is worth living,
and your belief will help create the fact.

~ William James

⌘

Look closely.
The beautiful may be small.

~ Immanuel Kant

⌘

Be patient and tough;
someday this pain will
be useful to you.

~ *Ovid*

⌘

Everything comes gradually
and at its appointed hour.

~ *Ovid*

⌘

Patience and diligence,
like faith, remove mountains.

~ *William Penn*

⌘

Time is the wisest of all counselors.

~ *Plutarch*

⌘

Never be ashamed to
admit what you do not know.

~ *Arabic Proverb*

⌘

Bless us, dark earth as we give back
that which we have received
as we make a forest of blessing a ridge of blessing
for the future to grow upon.

~ *Chinook Psalter*

⌘

One minute of patience, ten years of peace.

~ *Greek Proverb*

⌘

The soul does not live in the body as in a house,
but as in a tent, a place of temporary dwelling.

~ *Indian Proverb*

⌘

The salt of patience seasons everything.

~ *Italian Proverb*

⌘

The mountains, I become part of it…
The herbs, the fir tree, I become part of it.
The morning mists, the clouds,
the gathering waters, I become part of it…

~ *Navajo Chant*

⌘

All good things come to those who wait.

~ Proverb

⌘

Patience is the key to paradise.

~ Turkish Proverb

⌘

Patience with small details
makes perfect a large work,
like the universe.

~ Rumi

⌘

Luck is what happens when
preparation meets opportunity.

~ Seneca

⌘

More things are wrought by prayer
than this world dreams of.

~ Alfred Lord Tennyson

⌘

The two most powerful
warriors are patience and time.

~ Leo Tolstoy

⌘

Trying to understand is like
straining through muddy water.
Have the patience to wait!
Be still and allow the mud to settle.

~ Lao Tzu

⌘

Peaceful

Peaceful

True peace is not merely the absence of war,
it is the presence of justice.

~ Jane Addams

⌘

It is not enough to win a war;
it is more important to organize the peace.

~ Aristotle

⌘

By going within.
Nowhere you can go is more peaceful—
more free of interruptions—than your own soul.

~ Marcus Aurelius

⌘

A man is not called wise
because he talks and talks again;
but if he is peaceful, loving and fearless
then he is in truth called wise.

~ Buddha

⌘

Better than a thousand hollow words
is one word that brings peace.

~ *Buddha*

⌘

Peace comes from within, do not seek it without.

~ *Buddha*

⌘

Those who are free of resentful
thoughts surely find peace.

~ *Buddha*

⌘

Peace is liberty in tranquility.

~ *Cicero*

⌘

We shall find peace. We shall hear angels,
we shall see the sky sparkling with diamonds.

~ *Anton Chekhov*

⌘

Peace cannot be achieved through violence,
it can only be attained through understanding.

~ *Ralph Waldo Emerson*

⌘

No man is free who is not master of himself.
~ *Epictetus*

⌘

Silence is true wisdom's best reply.
~ *Euripides*

⌘

While you are proclaiming peace with your lips,
be careful to have it even more fully in your heart.
~ *St. Francis of Assisi*

⌘

He that would live in peace and at ease
must not speak all he knows or all he sees.
~ *Benjamin Franklin*

⌘

The lessons from the peace process are clear;
whatever life throws at us, our individual
responses will be all the stronger for
working together and sharing the load.
~ *Benjamin Franklin*

⌘

It is madness for sheep to
talk peace with a wolf.
~ *Thomas Fuller*

⌘

On all the peaks lies peace.
~ *Johann Wolfgang von Goethe*

⌘

A person should always
develop his ability to do goodness.
Make yourself better; this
should be every person's goal.
~ *Immanuel Kant*

⌘

For peace to reign on Earth,
humans must evolve into new beings
who have learned to see the whole first.
~ *Immanuel Kant*

⌘

Be a peacemaker in everyday life.
Display peace in everything you do.
Be peace. Live in peace.
~ *Buddhist Proverb*

⌘

If you want to live in peace,
you must not tell everything that you know,
nor judge everything that you see.

~ Mexican Proverb

⌘

With humbleness, kindness, and self-sacrifice,
you will take the weapon from any enemy.
Any fire dies if there is insufficient wood.

~ Buddhist Saying

⌘

Take rest; a field that has
rested gives a bountiful crop.

~ Ovid

⌘

Remember the entrance to
the sanctuary is inside you.

~ Rumi

⌘

The best fighter is never angry.

~ Lao Tzu

⌘

He who is contented is rich.

~ Lao Tzu

⌘

To a mind that is still the
whole universe surrenders.

~ Lao Tzu

⌘

To win one hundred victories in one
hundred battles is not the acme of skill.
To subdue the enemy without
fighting is the acme of skill.

~ Sun Tzu

⌘

Peace is not the absence of conflict,
but the ability to cope with it.

~ Author Unknown

⌘

Peace is always beautiful.

~ Walt Whitman

⌘

Purposeful

Chaos was the law of nature;
Order was the dream of man.

~ Henry Adams

⌘

Life is short.
Do not forget about the most
important things in our life,
living for other people and
doing good for them.

~ Marcus Aurelius

⌘

Look within. Within is the fountain of the good,
and it will ever bubble up, if you wilt ever dig.

~ Marcus Aurelius

⌘

Establish your purpose when you are
alone and without temptations.

~ Jeremy Bentham

⌘

Your purpose in life is to find your purpose
and give your whole heart and soul to it.

~ Buddha

⌘

A man does not know what he is saying
until he knows what he is not saying.

~ G.K. Chesterton

⌘

The best way to lengthen out our days
is to walk steadily and with a purpose.

~ Charles Dickens

⌘

The mystery of human existence
lies not in just staying alive,
but in finding something to live for.

~ Fyodor Dostoyevsky

⌘

Good luck is another name
for tenacity of purpose.

~ Ralph Waldo Emerson

⌘

Make your own Bible.
Select and collect all the words and
sentences that in all your readings have
been to you like the blast of a trumpet.

~ Ralph Waldo Emerson

⌘

The reward of a thing well done is to have done it.

~ Ralph Waldo Emerson

⌘

Daring ideas are like chessmen moved forward.
They may be beaten, but they may
start a winning game.

~ Johann Wolfgang von Goethe

⌘

The greatest thing in this world is
not so much where we stand as in
what direction we are moving.

~ Johann Wolfgang von Goethe

⌘

Make your work to be in
keeping with your purpose.

~ Leonardo da Vinci

⌘

The further any purpose the
faster we should work toward it.

~ Giuseppe Mazzini

⌘

He who has a why to live
can bear almost any how.

~ Friedrich Nietzsche

⌘

The measure of a man is
what he does with power.

~ Plato

⌘

Don't bite off more than you can chew.

~ Proverb

⌘

When walking, walk. When eating, eat.

~ Zen Proverb

⌘

Purposeful

Be a lamp, or a lifeboat, or a ladder.
Help someone's soul heal.
Walk out of your house like a shepherd.

~ Rumi

⌘

Everyone has been made for some
particular work and the desire for that
work has been put in every heart.

~ Rumi

⌘

Forget safety.
Live where you fear to live.
Destroy your reputation.
Be notorious.

~ Rumi

⌘

Out beyond ideas of wrongdoing
and rightdoing there is a field.
I'll meet you there.
When the soul lies down in that grass
the world is too full to talk about.

~ Rumi

⌘

When you do things from your soul,
you feel a river moving in you, a joy.

~ Rumi

⌘

Yesterday I was clever,
so I wanted to change the world.
Today I am wise,
so I am changing myself.

~ Rumi

⌘

Your task is not to seek for love,
but merely to seek and find all
the barriers within yourself that
you have built against it.

~ Rumi

⌘

It is not enough to be
a hardworking person.
Think: what do you work at?

~ Henry David Thoreau

⌘

It is not enough to be industrious;
so are the ants.
What are you industrious about?

~ Henry David Thoreau

⌘

Happy are those whose purpose has found them.

~ Author Unknown

⌘

It is wise to direct your
anger towards problems—
not people;
to focus your energies on answers—
not excuses.

~ William Arthur Ward

⌘

Resilient

Hold yourself responsible for a higher
standard than anybody else expects of you.
Never excuse yourself. Never pity yourself.
Be a hard master to yourself and
be lenient to everybody else.

~ Henry Ward Beecher

⌘

In our lives, change is unavoidable,
loss is unavoidable.
In the adaptability and ease with
which we experience change,
lies our happiness and freedom.

~ Buddha

⌘

No one saves us but ourselves.
No one can and no one may.
We ourselves must walk the path.

~ Buddha

⌘

Our greatest glory is not in never falling,
but in rising every time we fall.

~ Confucius

⌘

It is not the strongest of the species that survive,
nor the most intelligent,
but the one most responsive to change.

~ Charles Darwin

⌘

However, the Sun himself is
weak when he first rises,
and gathers strength and courage
as the day gets on.

~ Charles Dickens

⌘

There are dark shadows on the earth,
but its lights are stronger in the contrast.

~ Charles Dickens

⌘

It is easier to build strong children
than to repair broken men.

~ Frederick Douglass

⌘

The joy of your spirit is the indication of your strength.
~ *Ralph Waldo Emerson*

⌘

Some of us think holding on makes us strong;
but sometimes it is letting go.
~ *Hermann Hesse*

⌘

Adversity reveals genius.
~ *Horace*

⌘

The real man smiles in trouble,
gathers strength from distress,
and grows brave by reflection.
~ *Thomas Paine*

⌘

Look for the truth; it wants to be found.
~ *Blaisé Pascal*

⌘

Faith can move mountains.
~ *Proverb*

⌘

For there is no friend like a
sister in calm or stormy weather;
To cheer one on the tedious way,
to fetch one if one goes astray,
to lift one if one totters down,
to strengthen whilst one stands.

~ Christina Rossetti

⌘

Don't grieve.
Anything you lose comes
round in another form.

~ Rumi

⌘

The way to true knowledge does not go
through soft grass covered with flowers.
To find it, a person must climb
steep mountains.

~ John Ruskin

⌘

Most powerful is he who
has himself in his own power.

~ Seneca

⌘

A single twig breaks,
bundle of twigs is strong.

~ Tecumseh

⌘

When you rise in the morning,
give thanks for the morning light,
for your life, for strength.
Give thanks for your food
And the joy of living.

~ Tecumseh

⌘

What a man thinks of himself,
that it is which determines,
or rather indicates his fate.

~ Henry David Thoreau

⌘

Being deeply loved by
someone gives you strength,
while loving someone deeply
gives you courage.

~ Lao Tzu

⌘

Mastering others is strength,
mastering yourself is true power.

~ *Lao Tzu*

⌘

Don't let your past dictate who you are.
Let it be the lesson that strengthens
the person you will become.

~ *Author Unknown*

⌘

Loving yourself starts with liking yourself,
which starts with respecting yourself, which
starts with thinking of yourself in positive ways.

~ *Author Unknown*

⌘

Self-love, self-respect, self-worth…
there is a reason they all start with 'self'.
You cannot find them in anyone else.

~ *Author Unknown*

⌘

When things change inside you,
things change around you.

~ *Author Unknown*

⌘

Love many things, for therein lies the true strength,
and whosoever loves much performs much,
and can accomplish much,
and what is done in love is done well.

~ *Vincent van Gogh*

⌘

There are two ways of exerting one's strength:
one is pushing down, the other is pulling up.

~ *Booker T. Washington*

⌘

This too shall pass away.

~ *Ella Wheeler Wilcox*

⌘

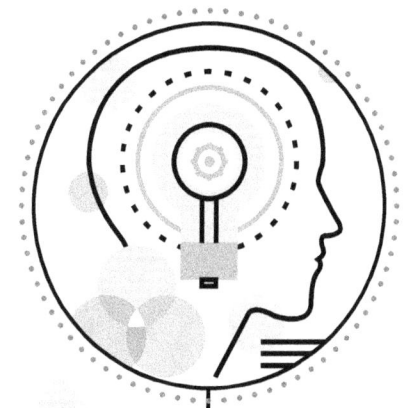

Thoughtful

Time in its aging course teaches all things.
~ *Aeschylus*

⌘

A tree is known by its fruit;
a man by his deeds.
A good deed is never lost;
he who sows courtesy reaps friendship,
and he who plants kindness gathers love.
~ *Saint Basil*

⌘

Gracious words are a honeycomb,
sweet to the soul and healing to the bones.
~ *Bible, Proverbs 16:23-25*

⌘

The mind is everything.
What you think you become.
~ *Buddha*

⌘

We are what we think.
All that we are arises with our thoughts.
With our thoughts, we make the world.

~ Buddha

⌘

Facts as fact do not always
create a spirit of reality,
because reality is a spirit.

~ G.K. Chesterton

⌘

Be attentive to what you do;
never consider anything
unworthy of your attention.

~ Confucius

⌘

If there were one word that could act
as a standard of conduct for one's entire life,
perhaps it would be thoughtfulness.

~ Confucius

⌘

Great thoughts come directly from the heart.

~ Luc de Clapiers

⌘

Conquer rage with humility,
conquer evil with goodness,
conquer greed with generosity,
and conquer lies with truth.

~ Dhammapada

⌘

I shall pass this way but once;
any good that I can do or any kindness
I can show to any human being;
let me do it now.
Let me not defer nor neglect it,
for I shall not pass this way again.

~ Stephen Grellet

⌘

You cannot step into the same river twice,
for other waters are continually flowing on.

~ Heraclitus

⌘

Three things in human life are important:
the first is to be kind; the second is to be kind;
and the third is to be kind.

~ Henry James

⌘

The reading of all good books is
like a conversation with the
finest minds of past centuries.
~ Immanuel Kant

⌘

Be happy for this moment.
This moment is your life.
~ Omar Khayyam

⌘

The thoughtful soul to solitude retires.
~ Omar Khayyam

⌘

I love those who can smile in trouble.
~ Leonardo da Vinci

⌘

The scholar who thinks but
does not create is like the cloud
which does not give rain.
~ Eastern Proverb

⌘

If you would like to know
how to recognize a prophet,
look to him who gives you the
knowledge of your own heart.

~ Persian Proverb

⌘

Actions speak louder than words.

~ Proverb

⌘

Do not seek pleasure everywhere,
but always be ready to find it.

~ John Ruskin

⌘

Good thoughts which originate from the hearts
of men as are useful as good examples.

~ Seneca

⌘

Have more than you show,
Speak less than you know.

~ William Shakespeare

⌘

Do not do to others what angers
you if done to you by others.

~ *Socrates*

⌘

When I stand before thee at the day's end,
thou shalt see my scars and know that
I had my wounds and also my healing.

~ *Rabindranath Tagore*

⌘

Repay evil with goodness.

~ *The Talmud*

⌘

I know of no more encouraging fact
than the unquestionable ability of man
to elevate his life by conscious endeavor.

~ *Henry David Thoreau*

⌘

Never look back unless you are
planning to go that way.

~ *Henry David Thoreau*

⌘

Things do not change; we change.

~ Henry David Thoreau

⌘

A saint lives with his inner life;
he denies outer life.

~ Lao Tzu

⌘

Kindness in words creates confidence.
Kindness in thinking creates profoundness.
Kindness in giving creates love.

~ Lao Tzu

⌘

Appendices

Favorite Meditation Quotes

Quote:_____
_____
_____
_____
_____

Quote:_____
_____
_____
_____
_____

Quote:_____
_____
_____
_____
_____

Quote:_____
_____
_____
_____
_____

The Little Book of Meditation Quotes

Quote:_____
_____
_____
_____
_____

Quote:_____
_____
_____
_____
_____

Quote:_____
_____
_____
_____
_____

Quote:_____
_____
_____
_____
_____

Appendix: Favorite Meditation Quotes

Quote:_____

_____

_____

_____

_____

Quote:_____

_____

_____

_____

_____

Quote:_____

_____

_____

_____

_____

Quote:_____

_____

_____

_____

_____

The Little Book of Meditation Quotes

Quote:_____

_____

_____

_____

_____

Quote:_____

_____

_____

_____

_____

Quote:_____

_____

_____

_____

_____

Quote:_____

_____

_____

_____

_____

Meditation Checklist

Aware
I find it...

_____
_____
_____
_____
_____
_____

Calm
I find it...

_____
_____
_____
_____
_____
_____

Creative
I find it...

_____
_____
_____
_____
_____
_____

Grateful
I find it...

___

Healthy
I find it...

___

Happy
I find it...

Hopeful
I find it...

_____

_____

_____

_____

_____

_____

Patient
I find it...

_____

_____

_____

_____

_____

_____

Peaceful
I find it...

_____

_____

_____

_____

_____

_____

Purpose
I find it...

Strength
I find it...

Thoughtful
I find it...

Other

I find it...

_____
_____
_____
_____
_____

Other

I find it...

_____
_____
_____
_____
_____

Other

I find it...

_____
_____
_____
_____
_____

Other
I find it...

_____

Other
I find it...

_____

Other
I find it...

Gratitude Journal

Things you discovered in...

January: _____

_____

_____

_____

_____

_____

_____

_____

February: _____

_____

_____

_____

_____

_____

_____

_____

March: _____

_____

_____

_____

_____

_____

_____

_____

Things you discovered in...

April: _____

_____

_____

_____

_____

_____

_____

May: _____

_____

_____

_____

_____

_____

_____

June: _____

_____

_____

_____

_____

_____

_____

Appendix: Meditation Journal

Things you discovered in...

July: _____

_____

_____

_____

_____

_____

_____

August: _____

_____

_____

_____

_____

_____

_____

September: _____

_____

_____

_____

_____

_____

_____

Things you discovered in...

October: _____

_____

_____

_____

_____

_____

_____

November: _____

_____

_____

_____

_____

_____

_____

December: _____

_____

_____

_____

_____

_____

_____

Biographical Index

Adams, Henry: 1838–1918, American historian
Adams, John Quincy: 1767 –1848, sixth president of the United States
Addams, Jane: 1860–1935, American settlement activist and author
Joseph Addison: 1672–1719, English essayist, poet, playwright, and politician
Aeschylus: 525–456 BC, Greek playwright
Aesop: c. 620–564 BCE, Greek storyteller
Alcott, Louisa May: 1832– 1888, American novelist, short story writer, and poet
Amiel, Henri Frédéric: 1821–1881, Swiss philosopher and poet
Aquinas, Thomas, Saint: 1225–1274, Dominican friar and Catholic priest
Aristotle: 384–322 BC, Greek philosopher
Augustine, Saint: 354–430, Theologian and philosopher
Aurelius, Marcus: 121–180, Roman Emperor

Bacon, Francis: 1561–1626, English philosopher
Baker, Richard St. Barbe: 1889–1982, English biologist and botanist
Basil, Saint: 329–379 AD, East Roman bishop
Beecher, Henry Ward: 1813–1887, American clergyman
Bentham, Jeremy: 1748–1832, English philosopher
Blake, William: 1757–1827, English poet
Boileau, Nicolas: 1636–1711, French poet and critic
Bonaparte, Napoleon: 1769–1821, French military and political leader
Buddha: 563–483 BC, Spiritual teacher
Burnett, Francis Hodgson: 1849–1924, British-American novelist and playwright
Burns, Robert: 1759–1796, Scottish poet

Cather, Willa: 1873–1947, American writer
Chaucer, Geoffrey: c. 1340s–1400, English poet and author
Chekhov, Anton: 1860–1904, Russian playwright and short-story writer
Chesterton, G.K. (Gilbert Keith): 1874–1936, English author
Cicero: 106–43 BC, Roman philosopher
Confucius: 551–479 BC, Chinese philosopher

Darwin, Charles: 1809–1882, English naturalist, geologist, and biologist
de Clapiers, Luc: 1715–1747, French writer and moralist
Descartes, René: 1596–1650, French mathematician
Dickens, Charles: 1812–1870, English novelist
Dickinson, Emily: 1830–1886, American poet
Disraeli, Benjamin: 1804–1881, British Prime Minister
Donne, John: 1572–1631, English poet
Dostoyevsky, Fyodor: 1821–1881, Russian novelist, philosopher, and short story writer
Douglass, Frederick: 1817–1895, American social reformer, abolitionist, orator, and writer
Dumas, Alexandre: 1802–1870, French writer

Eliot, George (Mary Ann Evans): 1819–1880, English novelist
Emerson, Ralph Waldo: 1803–1882, American writer and poet
Epictetus: 55–135 AD, Greek philosopher
Erasmus: 1466–1536, Dutch philosopher
Euripedes: 480–406 BC, Greek playwright

Francis of Assisi, Saint: 1181–1226, Italian preacher
Franklin, Benjamin: 1706–1790, American author and statesman
Fuller, Thomas: 1608–1661, English churchman and historian

Goethe, Johann Wolfgang von: 1749–1832, German writer
Grellet, Stephen: 1772–1855, French-American Quaker missionary

Hafez: 1315–1390, Persian poet
Hawthorne, Nathaniel: 1804–1864, American writer

Heraclitus: c.535–c.475 BC, Greek philosopher
Hesse, Hermann: 1877–1962, German-born Swiss poet, novelist, and painter
Hippocrates: c.460–c.370 BC, Greek physician
Hopkins, Gerard Manley: 1844–1889, English poet
Horace: 65–8 BC, Roman philosopher
Hubbard, Elbert: 1856–1915, American writer
Hugo, Victor: 1802–1885, French poet and novelist

James, Henry: 1843–1916, American author
James, William: 1842–1910, American philosopher
Johnson, Samuel: 1709–1784, English writer
Juvenal: 55–138 AD, Roman poet

Kant, Immanuel: 1724–1804, German philosopher
Khayyám, Omar: 1048–1131, Persian poet

Larcom, Lucy: 1824–1893, American teacher, poet, and author
Leonardo da Vinci: 1452–1519, Italian painter
Longfellow, Henry Wadsworth: 1807–1882, American poet
Lowell, James Russell: 1819–1891, American Romantic poet, critic, editor, and diplomat

Mazzini, Giuseppe: June 1805 – 10 March 1872), Italian politician, journalist, and activist
Michelangelo: 1475–1564, Italian sculptor, painter, and architect
Mozart: 1756–1791, prolific and influential composer

Nietzsche, Friedrich: 1844–1900, German philosopher

Ovid: 43 BC–17 AD, Roman poet

Paine, Thomas: 1737–1809, English-born American political activist
Pascal, Blasé: 1623–1662, French mathematician
Penn, William: 1644–1718, English writer
Plato: 428–348 BC, Greek philosopher
Plutarch: 46–120, Greek historian

Rossetti, Christina: 1830–1894, English poet
Ruskin, John: 1819–1900, English art critic
Rumi: 1207–1273, Persian poet

Seneca: c. 4 BC–AD 65, Roman philosopher
Shakespeare, William: 1564–1616, English poet and playwright
Shelley, Mary (Mary Wollstonecraft Godwin): 1797–1851, English writer
Shelley, Percy Bysshe: 1792–1822, English Romantic poet
Smiles, Samuel: 1812–1904, Scottish author
Socrates: 469–399 BC, Greek philosopher
Stevenson, Robert Louis: 1850–1894, Scottish novelist and poet
Syrus, Publilius: 85–43 BC, Latin writer

Tagore, Rabindranath: 1861–1941, Bengali poet
Tecumseh: c. 1768–1813, Shawnee chief and warrior
Tennyson, Alfred Lord: 1809–1892, English poet and writer
Thackeray, William Makepeace: 1811–1863, English novelist, author and illustrator
Thoreau, Henry David: 1817–1862, American writer and poet
Thucydides: c. 460–c. 400 BC, Greek historian and general
Tolstoy, Leo: 1828–1910, Russian writer
Tzu, Lao: 570–490 BC, Chinese philosopher
Tzu, Sun: c. 6th century BC, Chinese general and philosopher

van Gogh, Vincent: 1853–1890, Dutch post-impressionist painter
Voltaire: 1694–1778, French writer

Ward, William Arthur: 1921–1994, American writer
Washington, Booker T.: 1856–1915, American educator, author, and orator
Whitman, Walt: 1819–1892, American poet
Wilcox, Ella Wheeler: 1850–1919, American writer and poet
Wilde, Oscar: 1854–1900, Irish writer
Wordsworth, William: 1770–1850, English poet

Index

Adams, Henry: 81
Adams, John Quincy: 63
Addams, Jane: 73
Joseph Addison: 45
Aeschylus: 101
Aesop: 27
Alcott, Louisa May: 35
Amiel, Henri Frédéric: 19, 27
Aquinas, Thomas, Saint: 11
Aristotle: 3, 27, 35, 63, 73
Augustine, Saint: 63
Aurelius, Marcus: 3, 11, 19, 35, 36, 63, 73, 81

Bacon, Francis: 4
Baker, Richard St. Barbe: 11
Basil, Saint: 101
Beecher, Henry Ward: 19, 45, 91
Bentham, Jeremy: 81
Bible: 4, 12, 28, 55, 101
Blake, William: 4
Boileau, Nicolas: 64
Bonaparte, Napoleon: 55
Buddha: 4, 12, 36, 45, 73, 74, 82, 91, 101, 102
Burnett, Francis Hodgson: 56
Burns, Robert: 56

Cather, Willa: 12
Chaucer, Geoffrey: 64
Chekhov, Anton: 74
Chesterton, G.K. (Gilbert Keith): 37, 56, 82, 102
Cicero: 13, 46, 56, 74
Confucius: 28, 37, 56, 57, 102

Darwin, Charles: 92
de Clapiers, Luc: 102
Descartes, René: 44
Dhammapada: 103
Dickens, Charles: 37, 57, 82, 92
Dickinson, Emily: 57
Disraeli, Benjamin: 37, 57
Donne, John: 13
Dostoyevsky, Fyodor: 57, 82
Douglass, Frederick: 92
Dumas, Alexandre: 4

Eliot, George (Mary Ann Evans): 5, 28
Emerson, Ralph Waldo: 5, 13, 19, 20, 29, 38, 58, 64, 74, 82, 83, 93
Epictetus: 5, 6, 38, 58, 75
Erasmus: 46
Euripedes: 13, 29, 75

Francis of Assisi, Saint: 38, 75
Franklin, Benjamin: 38, 64, 75
Fuller, Thomas: 58, 76

Goethe, Johann Wolfgang von: 20, 58, 64, 76, 83
Grellet, Stephen: 103

Hafez: 6, 20, 29
Hawthorne, Nathaniel: 38
Heraclitus: 64, 103
Hesse, Hermann: 14, 20, 93
Hippocrates: 46
Hopkins, Gerard Manley: 64
Horace: 93
Hubbard, Elbert: 29, 58
Hugo, Victor: 14, 21, 29, 58

James, Henry: 103
James, William: 30, 47, 65
Johnson, Samuel: 59
Juvenal: 47

Kant, Immanuel: 59, 65, 76, 104
Khayyám, Omar: 104

Larcom, Lucy: 59
Leonardo da Vinci: 6, 21, 83, 104
Longfellow, Henry Wadsworth: 59
Lowell, James Russell: 21

Mantras: 30
Mazzini, Giuseppe: 84
Michelangelo: 21
Mozart: 22

Nietzsche, Friedrich: 6, 22, 30, 84

Ovid: 66, 77

Paine, Thomas: 93
Pascal, Blaisé: 93
Penn, William: 66
Plato: 14, 47, 84
Plutarch: 66
Proverbs: 6, 7, 14, 15, 39, 47, 48, 59, 60, 66, 67, 68, 76, 77, 84, 93, 104, 105

Rossetti, Christina: 15, 94
Ruskin, John: 94, 105
Rumi: 7, 15, 16, 22, 31, 49, 68, 77, 84, 85, 86, 94

Seneca: 22, 23, 31, 39, 68, 94, 105
Shakespeare, William: 31, 49, 50, 105
Shelley, Mary (Mary Wollstonecraft Godwin): 23
Shelley, Percy Bysshe: 60
Smiles, Samuel: 40
Socrates: 50, 106
Stevenson, Robert Louis: 23
Syrus, Publilius: 50

Tagore, Rabindranath: 31, 106
Talmud: 106
Tecumseh: 95
Tennyson, Alfred Lord: 60, 68
Thackeray, William Makepeace: 7, 32
Thoreau, Henry David: 7, 32, 50, 60, 86, 95, 106, 107
Thucydides: 16
Tolstoy, Leo: 8, 16, 23, 40, 68

Tzu, Lao: 8, 16, 51, 69, 77, 78, 95, 96, 106, 107
Tzu, Sun: 78

Author Unknown: 8, 23, 31, 40, 41, 60, 78, 96

van Gogh, Vincent: 23, 24, 97
da Vinci, Leonardo: 6, 21, 83, 104
Voltaire: 31, 51

Ward, William Arthur: 24, 41, 87
Washington, Booker T.: 97
Whitman, Walt: 8, 78
Wilcox, Ella Wheeler: 97
Wilde, Oscar: 24
Wordsworth, William: 24, 32

About the Editor

Kathleen Welton is an award-winning editor, publisher, and writer with more than 40 years of experience in content areas including business and finance, legal, lifestyle, reference, and self-help.

She began her book publishing career as a Sales Representative for D. Van Nostrand. She has since served in a variety of editorial and publishing roles including Senior Editor for Dow Jones-Irwin, VP & Publisher for Dearborn Trade, VP & Publisher for IDG Books, and Director of Book Publishing for the American Bar Association. She is currently a Book Producer with aka Associates.

Her books include *The Little Book of Gratitude Quotes*, *The Little Book of Meditation Quotes*, *The Little Book of Quotes by Women* and *The Little Book of Success Quotes*.

The Little Quote Books series has been recognized with awards including USA Book News Award (Winner) for *The Little Book of Humorous Quotes* and USA Book News Award (Finalist) for *The Little Book of Gratitude Quotes* and *The Little Book of Horse Quotes*.

Kathleen graduated from Stanford University with a BA in both English and Italian.

She serves as an avid advocate for beaches, birds, and wildlife.

The Little Quote Books Series

The Little Book of Gratitude Quotes
The Little Book of Horse Quotes
The Little Book of Humorous Quotes
The Little Book of Meditation Quotes
The Little Book of Quotes by Women
The Little Book of Success Quotes

www.ingramcontent.com/pod-product-compliance
Lightning Source LLC
Chambersburg PA
CBHW072337300426
44109CB00042B/1666